DRUMS
50 Solos for Drumset

by
Ben Hans

T0052942

ISBN 978-0-634-04015-3

HAL•LEONARD®
CORPORATION

7777 W. BLUEMOUND RD. P.O. BOX 13819 MILWAUKEE, WI 53213

Visit Hal Leonard Online at
www.halleonard.com

Dedication

This book is dedicated to two of my favorite drummers:

EVAN FISHER

My first teacher, inspiration, and mentor… thank you.

BILLY HIGGINS

An inspiration for all of us, and for many more generations of drummers to follow… farewell and God bless.

Ackowledgments

I would not be able to call music and drumming my life and ambition without the help of the following special people: my wife Dawn, for her friendship, love, advice, and never-ending support of my musical adventures; my parents Ralph and Sandra Hans for all the years of encouraging my music habit; my fantastic teachers through the years, Evan Fisher, Vicki Jenks, Terry Smirl, Bob Hobbs, John Broecker, John Becker, Ernie Adams, Jack Grassel; and all the great musicians I am fortunate enough to play with that allow me to pay the bills. Thank you to all of my music students, you are now my constant source of inspiration.

Also, special thanks to Jim Catalano at Ludwig for his assistance, to Diana Banes and Rachel Donnelly for their talented support, and to Rick Mattingly and the crew at Hal Leonard Corporation—thanks for making this project a reality.

Table of Contents

About the Author

BEN HANS is a musician and music instructor in the greater Milwaukee area. He keeps a busy performance schedule throughout the Upper Midwest, teaches music classes and percussion studies at Milwaukee Area Technical College, and instructs more than 60 private music students as well as the West Bend High School drum line. In addition to leading his own jazz trio, Ben performs or has performed with the following: Chuck Hedges Swingtet, Jack Grassel, Barry Harris, James Dallas, Jeff Schroedl, Jazz Force Five, Swing Nouveau, the Bruce Russell Band, the Surf Boys, Swingset Police, and various musical theatre orchestras. An active member of the Percussive Arts Society, Ben holds an associates degree in music from Milwaukee Area Technical College, and a bachelor's degree in music from the University of Wisconsin.

*AUTHOR'S NOTE: Any comments or questions regarding the music content of this book would be graciously received and promptly answered. Contact the author via the internet at **www.benhans.com***

Preface

As most musicians will honestly tell you, the trade of making music is that of a constant personal growth and evolution. Working musicians are always trying to better themselves through performance, practice, and persistence. So although it may not be evident, most of us are always working out something. As drummers, we are constantly trying to find the next great groove, pattern, sticking, or way of developing our chops to have hands and feet moving in ways that were thought impossible only a few days, weeks, or months before.

This book is a collection of musical "ideas" for the drumset, which gradually become more difficult as you work through them. These ideas are simply drumming "snapshots" of *some* styles of music. This book is not an end in itself. As an evolving musician, you must play music, improvise, study, and constantly have your ears open to *all kinds of music*. It is sometimes too easy to get into a rut, hit a wall, and not progress. Yes, it happens to the best of us. Do not give up. Try to vary your practice routines and the styles of music you are studying. Sometimes as drummers, we may feel and play music in just a few styles. It is often too easy to label one's drumming: "I'm a rock drummer," "She's a Jazz drummer," "He's a country drummer," and so forth. Always try to broaden your musical perspective. There is so much wonderful music in the world to be appreciated, do yourself a favor and start listening to it. For many practicing musicians, this is a large part of their inspiration. As long as you practice consistently, allow yourself to explore and learn about varied styles and types of music, have open ears and an open mind, you will progress.

This is the concept behind *Workin' Drums*, because at any level we are all still "workin' it out."

How to Use This Book

This collection of solo drumset music is written to provide the practicing drummer with some interesting "ideas" to explore through a varied selection of musical styles and degrees of difficulty. It also will assist the practicing drummer to acquire a better knowledge of form, dynamics, music terminology, and overall musicianship. This work can be used as a lesson supplement, or as performance material for recitals and solo competitions.

This is not a method book. It is meant to accompany a study of the snare drum and introduction to drumset. If you are not versed in these topics, find a teacher in your area who can help you develop the skills needed to work through these pieces. If you find a style of drumming you are not familiar with, enjoy greatly, or become frustrated with, investigate it vigorously through listening to music and obtaining other drumming books on the subject. At this point in time, there are so many great books available to study; take advantage of it. (Still stumped? Start at www.halleonard.com.)

This book is written for a five-piece drumset voicing, which is currently the most familiar and basic setup of the standard student drumset. This would include a snare drum, a bass drum, high, middle, and low toms (as well as hi-hat, ride, and crash cymbals). If you have a four-piece drumset, simply move the middle tom voice to the high tom. If you have a bigger setup, feel free to use other voicings for drums and cymbals around your kit. The drumming police will not come to your house.

Always use a metronome. When first playing these solos, set the metronome 20 to 40 b.p.m. slower than the given tempo. Work up to the given tempo marking before you progress to the next selection. When you have completed each study, feel free to improvise in the style of each example. This is how new ideas are created!

Practice regularly. Set up a practice routine, or keep a practice journal. Be dedicated and persistent. Without constant practice, it is impossible to improve on your instrument!

Always listen. Don't just hear the music. Listen to the drummer on your favorite recordings. Go to your public library or go online to find new music in all genres. Go to concerts, watch drumming videos. Find your own ways to stay excited about drumming.

Have fun! That's why we all picked up the sticks in the first place, right?

Notation Legend
Five Piece Drumset

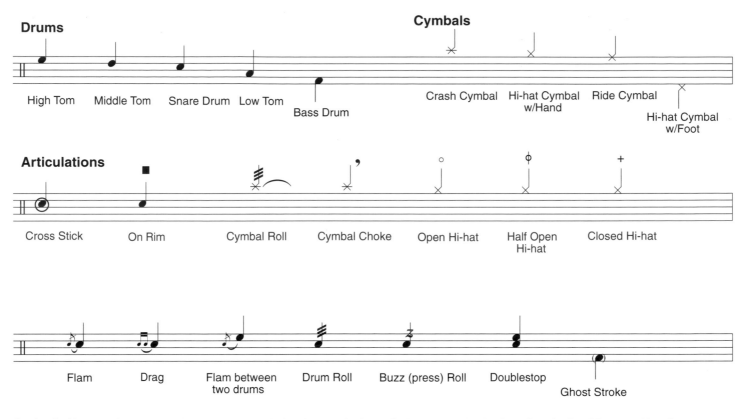

Author's Note: This notation legend is modeled after the standards set forth in the work: *Guide to Standardized Drumset Notation*, by Norman Weinberg, published by the Percussive Arts Society, 1998. It is the author's opinion that this is the most comprehensive work of its kind available to this date, and if future publications also conformed to this notation system, reading drumset notation would be much easier.

Gettin' Started

Warmin' Up

Turn the Corner

Lazy Days

The Usual Suspects

Four on the Floor

Simply Swing

Feelin' the Three

All Together Now

Some Crazy Stuff

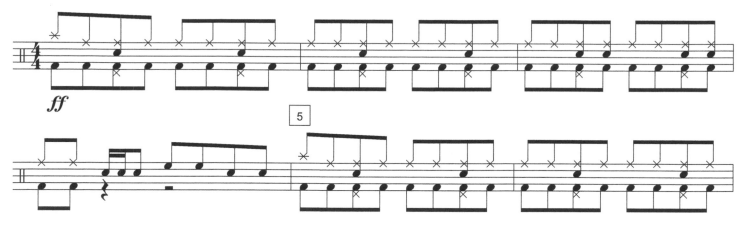

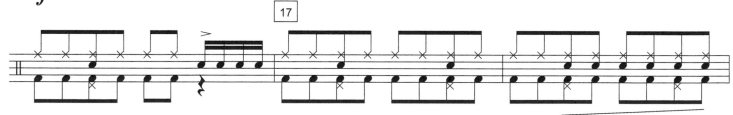

One for Liberty

First and Twelve

On the Bubble

Ride It

Hear Together

♩=78

Fill 'er Up

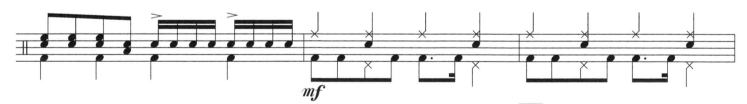

Big Reach

A Swingin' Waltz

♩= 104-124

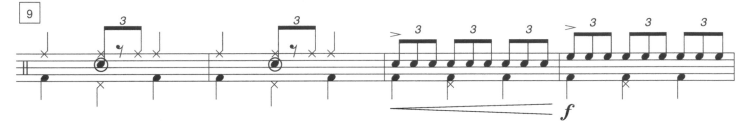

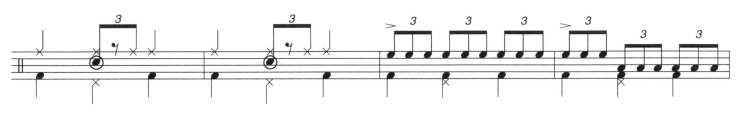

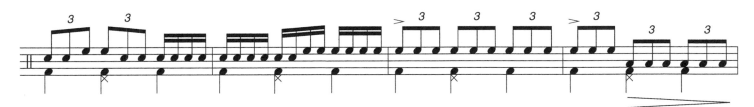

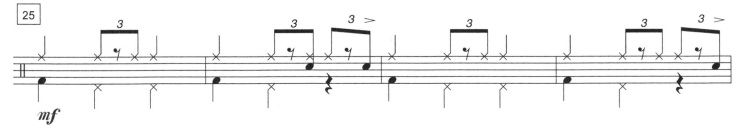

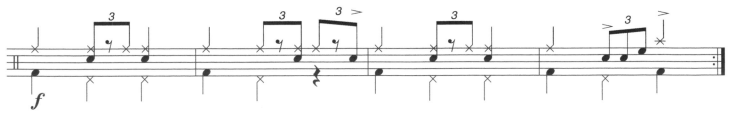

12 A.M.

Up the Ladder

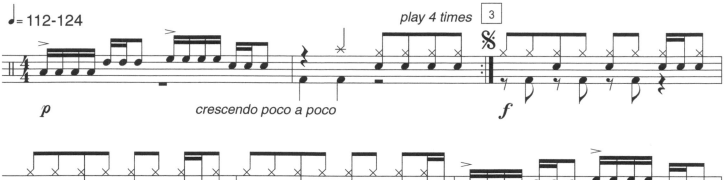

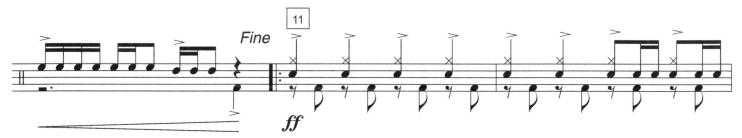

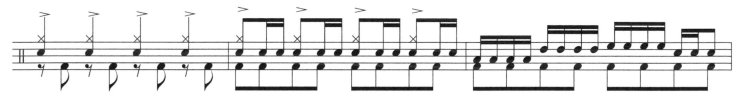

So the Story Goes...

$\quad$ = 104-118

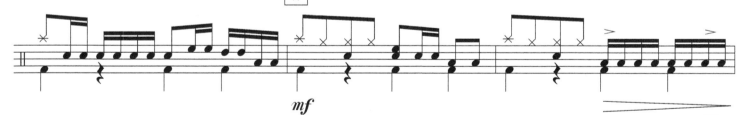

Big Groove

Five and Dime

Chicago Shufflin'

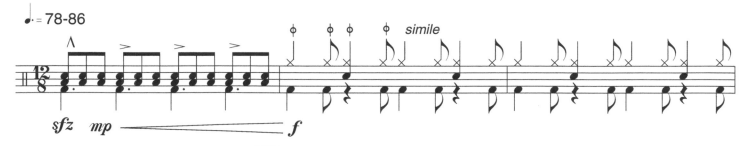

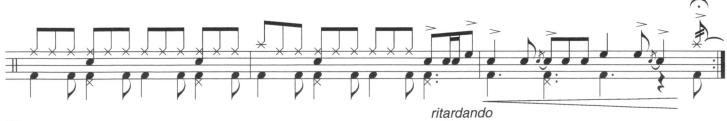

Movin' On

♩= 70-82

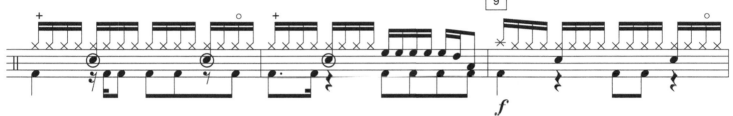

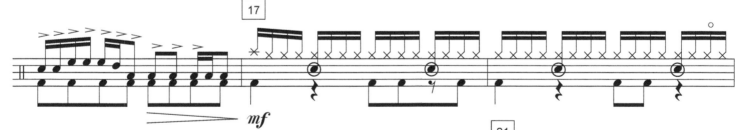

Goin' Around

♩=100

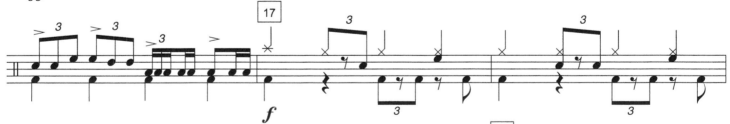

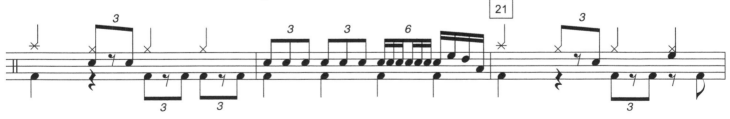

Breakdown

El Gato

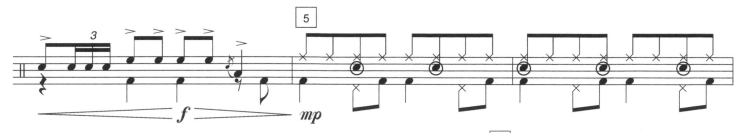

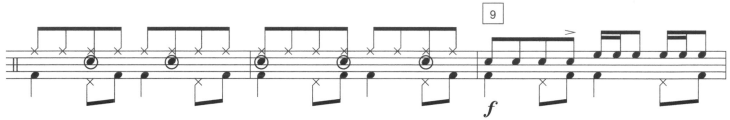

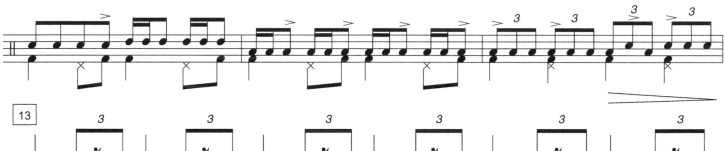

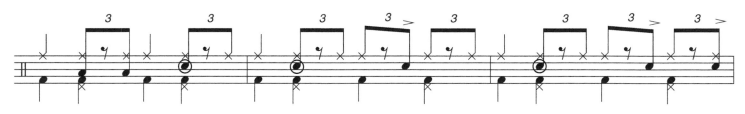

Bring It

$\quad$ = 94-100

Transit

Supernova

Big Band Swinger

Trainin'

Time Frame

Heavy

♩ = 96

Shut the Door

Up Front

Sixteenth Frenzy

♩=104-116

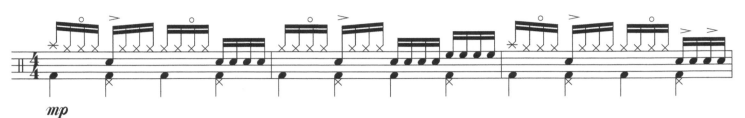

mp

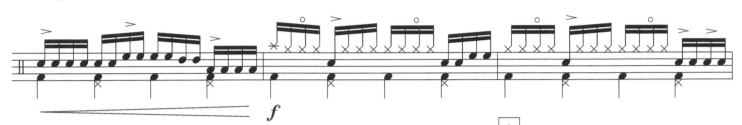

f

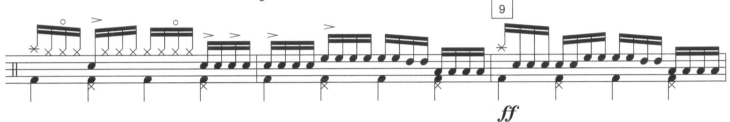

9

ff

mp

13

crescendo poco a poco

21

ff

mf

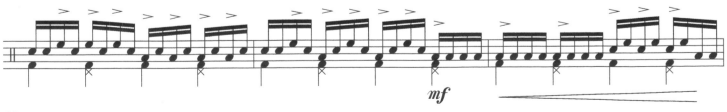

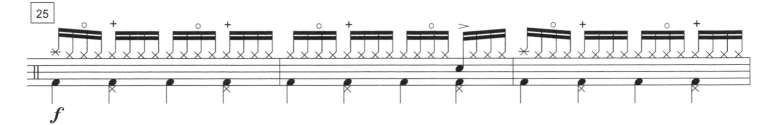

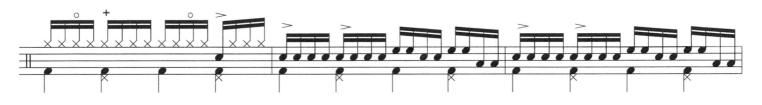

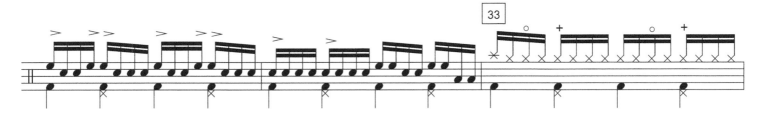

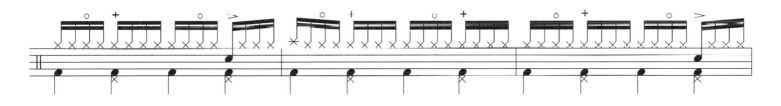

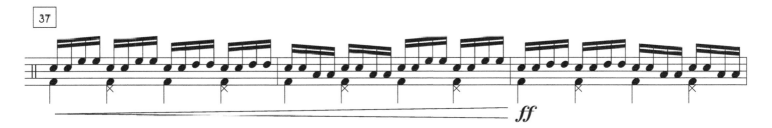

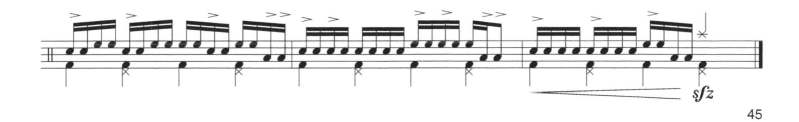

One for Evan

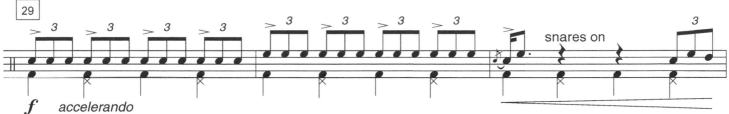

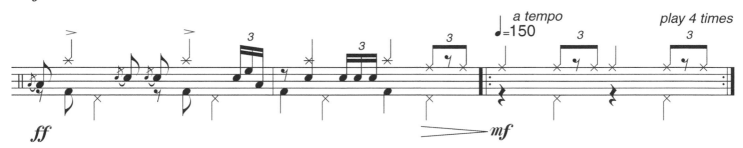

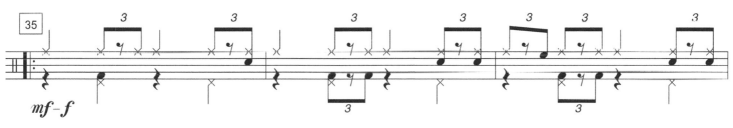

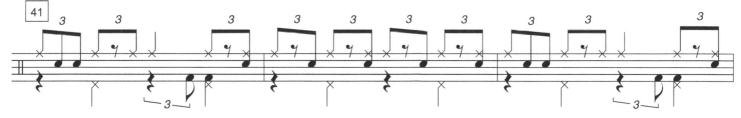

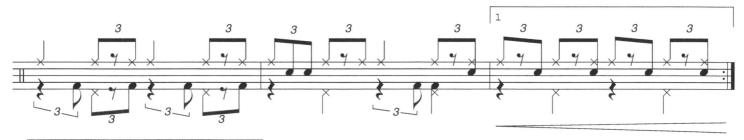

Struttin' in Nawlins

Bending

♩ = 92-98

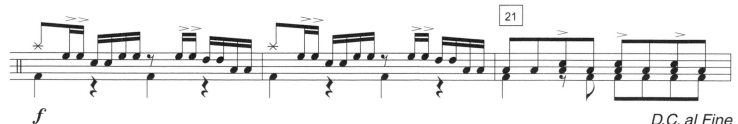

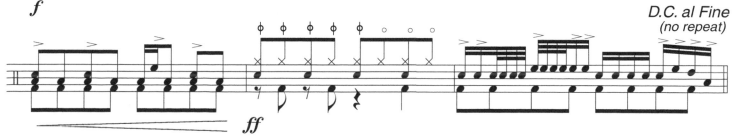

The Key

Bajan Holiday

♩=108-116

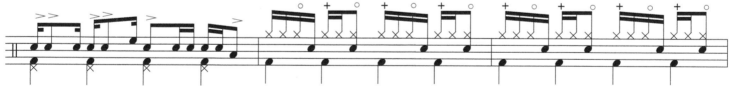

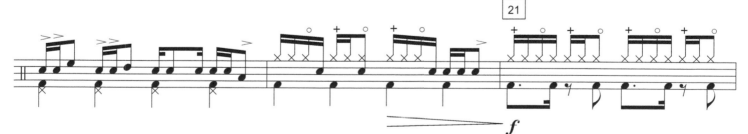

Triplet Frenzy

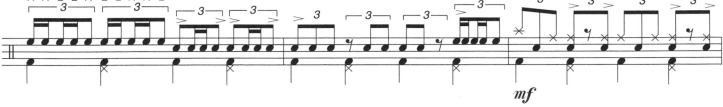

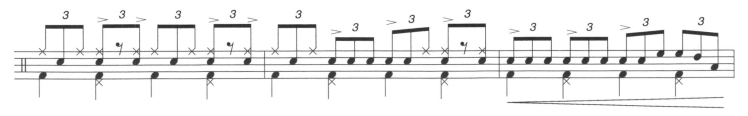

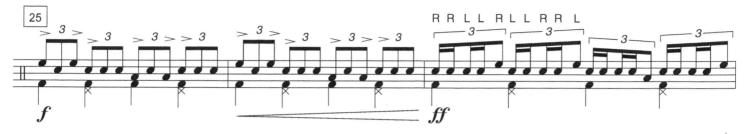

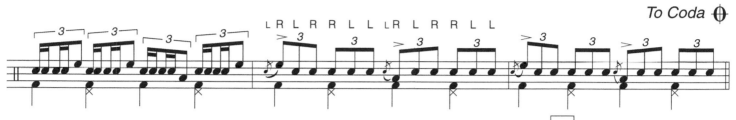

To Coda ⊕

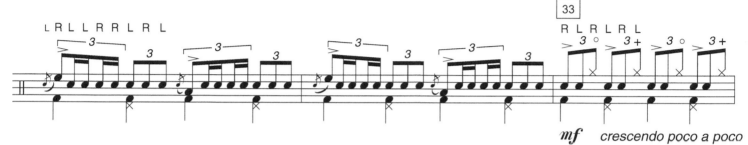

33

mf *crescendo poco a poco*

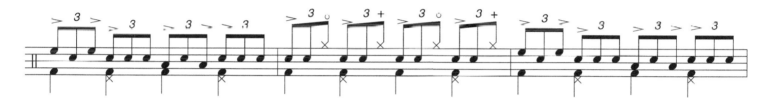

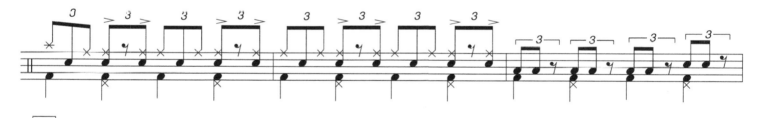

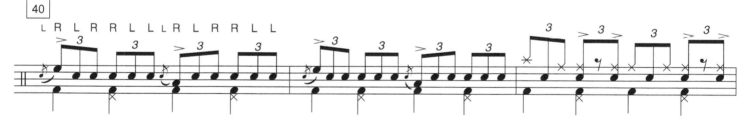

40

D.S. al Coda

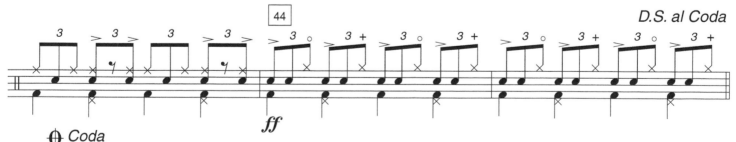

44

ff

⊕ Coda

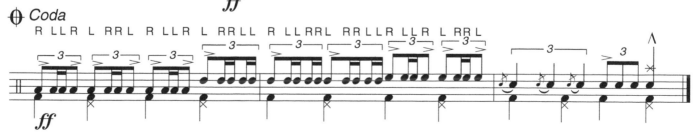

ff

Reggae Kick

Workin'

Swingin' for Billy

♩ = 130-144

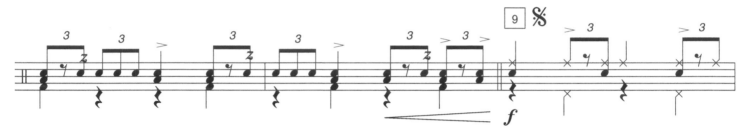

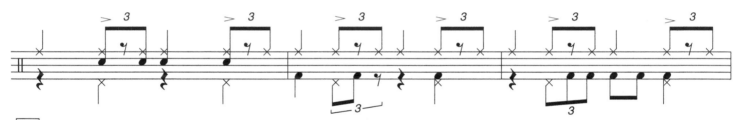

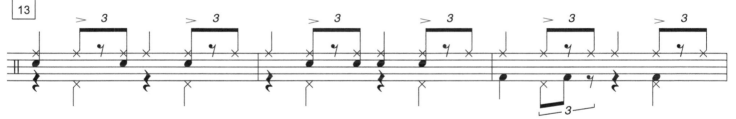

*Performance note - Play measures 41-44 on rim of snare drum with stick tip facing upwards, move stick up and down on rim between fulcrum and shoulder of stick to produce pitch change or "flange" effect.

Supercharger

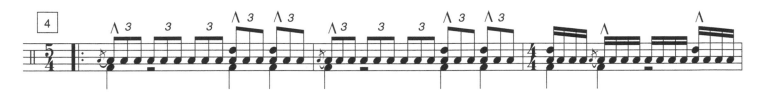

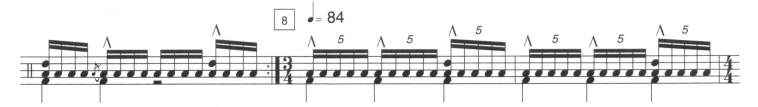

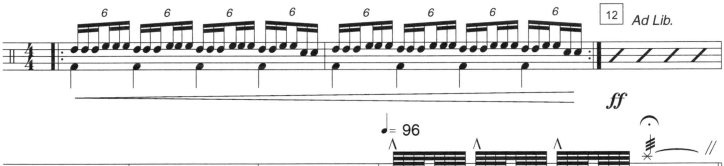

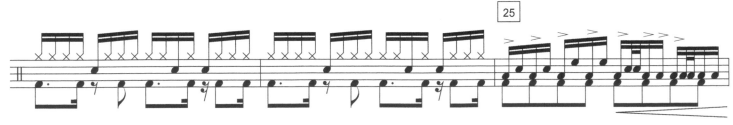

f

To Coda ⊕

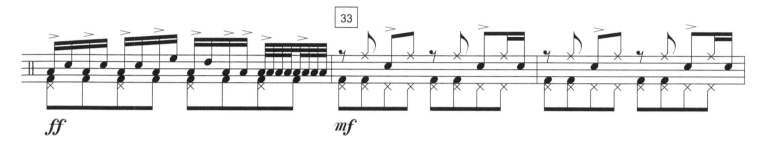

33

$f\!f$ mf

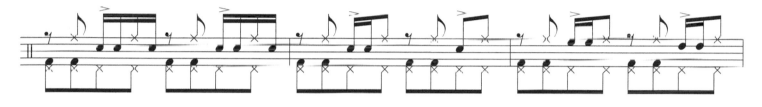

f

D.S. al Coda

44 ⌀ ⌀ ⌀ *simile* + +

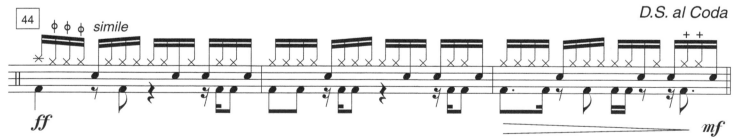

$f\!f$ mf

Coda
⊕

$f\!f$ *ritardando*

Turbulence

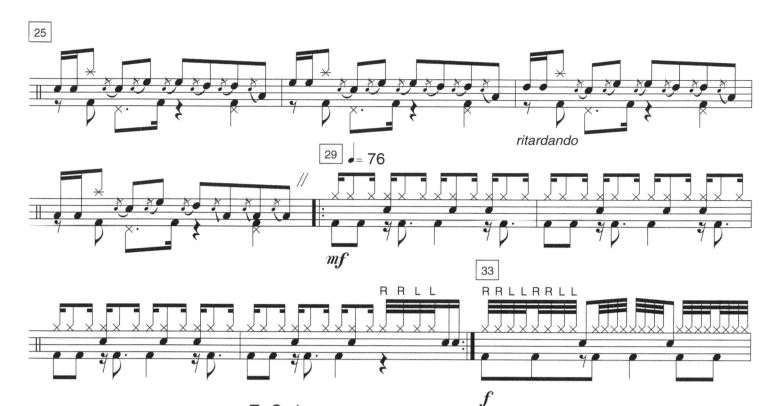

ritardando

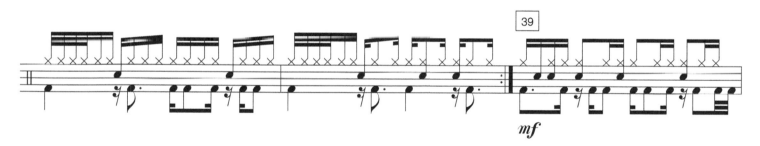

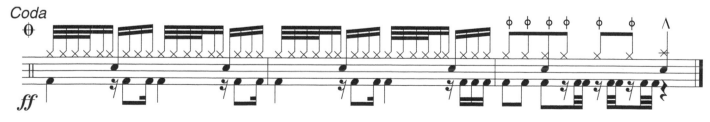

Twelfth Floor

Glossary

Music terms and articulations used in this book

Terms

accelerando	Gradually faster
Ad Lib.	Improvise, make up your own part within the music, go for it!
a tempo	Return to original tempo or rate of speed
crescendo	⟍ Gradually louder
decrescendo	⟋ Gradually softer
poco a poco	Little by little
ritardando	Gradually slower
simile	Continue in the same manner, style

Articulations

>	Accent	Play note with stong attack
∧	Marcato	Loud emphasized accent
·	Staccato	Short, detached
⌢·	Fermata	Hold out
//	Break (Railroad Tracks)	Short pause

Dynamics

pp	Pianissimo	Very soft
p	Piano	Soft
mp	Mezzo piano	Moderately soft
mf	Mezzo forte	Moderately loud
f	Forte	Loud
ff	Fortissimo	Very loud
fff	Fortississimo	Very very loud
sfz	Sforzando	Special stress and sudden emphasis

Repeat terms and signs

D.C. (Da Capo)	Return to the beginning
D.S. (Dal Segno)	Return to the sign (𝄋)
Fine	End or close
𝄋	Section repeat sign
⨁	Coda sign, ending of an arrangement
D.C. al Fine	Da Capo, return to the beginning, play to fine
D.S. al Fine	Dal Segno, return to the sign (𝄋), play to fine
D.C. al Coda	Da Capo, return to the beginning, play to the coda sign (⨁), and skip to the coda
D.S. al Coda	Dal Segno, return to the sign (𝄋), play to the coda sign (⨁), skip to coda
play 4 times	Repeat as indicated

First ending (repeat, take second ending)

♩ = Metronome marking   2 ←Measure number   1

Neutral clef (percussion clef)   Slash notation (keep time in a similar style)   Bar Line   Music Staff   Repeat sign

Time Signature

YOU CAN'T BEAT OUR DRUM BOOKS!

Bass Drum Control
Best Seller for More Than 50 Years!
by Colin Bailey
This perennial favorite among drummers helps players develop their bass drum technique and increase their flexibility through the mastery of exercises.
06620020 Book/Online Audio $17.99

The Complete Drumset Rudiments
by Peter Magadini
Use your imagination to incorporate these rudimental etudes into new patterns that you can apply to the drumset or tom toms as you develop your hand technique with the Snare Drum Rudiments, your hand and foot technique with the Drumset Rudiments and your polyrhythmic technique with the Polyrhythm Rudiments. Adopt them all into your own creative expressions based on ideas you come up with while practicing.
06620016 Book/CD Pack $14.95

Drum Aerobics
by Andy Ziker
A 52-week, one-exercise-per-day workout program for developing, improving, and maintaining drum technique. Players of all levels – beginners to advanced – will increase their speed, coordination, dexterity and accuracy. The online audio contains all 365 workout licks, plus play-along grooves in styles including rock, blues, jazz, heavy metal, reggae, funk, calypso, bossa nova, march, mambo, New Orleans 2nd Line, and lots more!
06620137 Book/Online Audio $19.99

Drumming the Easy Way!
The Beginner's Guide to Playing Drums
for Students and Teachers
by Tom Hapke
Cherry Lane Music
Now with online audio! This book takes the beginning drummer through the paces – from reading simple exercises to playing great grooves and fills. Each lesson includes a preparatory exercise and a solo. Concepts and rhythms are introduced one at a time, so growth is natural and easy. Features large, clear musical print, intensive treatment of each individual drum figure, solos following each exercise to motivate students, and more!
02500876 Book/Online Audio...$19.99
02500191 Book..$14.99

The Drumset Musician – 2nd Edition
by Rod Morgenstein and Rick Mattingly
Containing hundreds of practical, usable beats and fills, *The Drumset Musician* teaches you how to apply a variety of patterns and grooves to the actual performance of songs. The accompanying online audio includes demos as well as 18 play-along tracks covering a wide range of rock, blues and pop styles, with detailed instructions on how to create exciting, solid drum parts.
00268369 Book/Online Audio.................................. $19.99

HAL•LEONARD®
www.halleonard.com

Instant Guide to Drum Grooves
The Essential Reference
for the Working Drummer
by Maria Martinez
Become a more versatile drumset player! From traditional Dixieland to cutting-edge hip-hop, *Instant Guide to Drum Grooves* is a handy source featuring 100 patterns that will prepare working drummers for the stylistic variety of modern gigs. The book includes essential beats and grooves in such styles as: jazz, shuffle, country, rock, funk, New Orleans, reggae, calypso, Brazilian and Latin.
06620056 Book/CD Pack $12.99

1001 Drum Grooves
The Complete Resource for Every Drummer
by Steve Mansfield
Cherry Lane Music
This book presents 1,001 drumset beats played in a variety of musical styles, past and present. It's ideal for beginners seeking a well-organized, easy-to-follow encyclopedia of drum grooves, as well as consummate professionals who want to bring their knowledge of various drum styles to new heights. Author Steve Mansfield presents: rock and funk grooves, blues and jazz grooves, ethnic grooves, Afro-Cuban and Caribbean grooves, and much more.
02500337 Book...$14.99

Polyrhythms – The Musician's Guide
by Peter Magadini
edited by Wanda Sykes
Peter Magadini's *Polyrhythms* is acclaimed the world over and has been hailed by *Modern Drummer* magazine as "by far the best book on the subject." Written for instrumentalists and vocalists alike, this book with online audio contains excellent solos and exercises that feature polyrhythmic concepts. Topics covered include: 6 over 4, 5 over 4, 7 over 4, 3 over 4, 11 over 4, and other rhythmic ratios; combining various polyrhythms; polyrhythmic time signatures; and much more. The audio includes demos of the exercises and is accessed online using the unique code in each book.
06620053 Book/Online Audio...$19.99

Joe Porcaro's Drumset Method – Groovin' with Rudiments
Patterns Applied to Rock, Jazz & Latin Drumset
by Joe Porcaro
Master teacher Joe Porcaro presents rudiments at the drumset in this sensational new edition of *Groovin' with Rudiments*. This book is chock full of exciting drum grooves, sticking patterns, fills, polyrhythmic adaptations, odd meters, and fantastic solo ideas in jazz, rock, and Latin feels. The online audio features 99 audio clip examples in many styles to round out this true collection of superb drumming material for every serious drumset performer.
06620129 Book/Online Audio $24.99

66 Drum Solos for the Modern Drummer
Rock • Funk • Blues • Fusion • Jazz
by Tom Hapke
Cherry Lane Music
66 Drum Solos for the Modern Drummer presents drum solos in all styles of music in an easy-to-read format. These solos are designed to help improve your technique, independence, improvisational skills, and reading ability on the drums and at the same time provide you with some cool licks that you can use right away in your own playing.
02500319 Book/Online Audio...$17.99

Prices, contents, and availability subject to change without notice.